INTERMEDIATE JAZZ
PIANO SOLOING

Solo With Extended Arpeggios, Chromatics, Bebop Extensions, Modes & Pentatonic Substitutions

NATHAN **HAYWARD**

FUNDAMENTAL**CHANGES**

Intermediate Jazz Piano Soloing

Solo With Extended Arpeggios, Chromatics, Bebop Extensions, Modes & Pentatonic Substitutions

ISBN: 978-1-78933-451-7

Published by **www.fundamental-changes.com**

Copyright © 2025 Nathan Hayward

Edited by Joseph Alexander & Tim Pettingale

www.fundamental-changes.com

Join our free Facebook Community of Cool Musicians

www.facebook.com/groups/fundamentalguitar

Instagram: **FundamentalChanges**

Cover Image Copyright: Shutterstock

Contents

Introduction

It's often said that jazz soloing is a language, and if you're reading this book then you are on your way to becoming a more articulate speaker.

Maybe you already know some of the "words" and stock phrases, but you're not sure about the grammar and correct usage? The challenge most people find with any language is to grasp its nuances and truly express themselves. For example, when you hear a joke in a language you're new to, everyone else might laugh, but you still need it explained. Once you understand the language, however, you get it – and you can also begin to make up your own jokes.

This book will expand your knowledge of the language of jazz piano, both in terms of the essential vocabulary, and the most important improvisation concepts you need to know – the ideas you'll draw upon time and again. Gradually, you'll become fluent in this language and be capable of translating these new sounds in exciting solos in real time.

In this book, we'll build on the foundation laid in the first book in this series, *Beginner Jazz Piano Soloing*. It's not essential to have read that book if you already have a grasp of the basics of jazz piano, but if any of the concepts here mystify you, it's probably worth getting hold of a copy and working your way through it.

Here, we will explore how to add chromatic passing notes to phrases to create the staple bebop jazz soloing vocabulary. We'll also look at how to alter extended chord tones (like the 9th, 13th and 11th) to create more interesting tensions when soloing over chords. Plus, we'll touch on modal and advanced pentatonic scale ideas.

Each chapter will introduce a concept with an in-depth explanation and dozens of licks to learn. You'll then be shown how to create some of your own ideas using each concept and learn a tune or a solo based on the idea. This process will quickly expand your soloing vocabulary and embed each concept so you can use it spontaneously in a solo.

Understanding and combining these different approaches will help you become an accomplished and creative improviser and lay a solid foundation for creating even more articulate ideas in the future.

True mastery only comes from diving deep into a subject, dedicating time to practice, immersing yourself in it, and integrating it into your life over a significant period of time. It's a fun process, but one that requires commitment and promises substantial rewards if you persevere.

This book will guide you and offer direction as you explore creatively and expand your jazz soloing vocabulary. I hope you enjoy the process, have fun playing along with the backing tracks, learn and invent new licks, and explore fresh ideas.

Have fun!

Nathan

Get the Audio

The audio files for this book are available to download for free from **www.fundamental-changes.com**. The link is in the top right-hand corner. Click Download Audio and choose your piano. Select the title of this book from the menu, and complete the form to get your audio.

We recommend that you download the files directly to your computer (not to your tablet or phone) and extract them there before adding them to your media library. If you encounter any difficulty, we provide technical support within 24 hours via the contact form.

For over 350 free guitar lessons with videos check out:

www.fundamental-changes.com

Join our free Facebook Community of Cool Musicians

www.facebook.com/groups/fundamentalguitar

Tag us for a share on Instagram: **FundamentalChanges**

Chapter One: Chromatic Passing Notes and Runs

We'll begin by exploring how chromatic passing notes and chromatic runs combine to create the distinctive sound of jazz. Chromatics are a foundational concept in jazz and immediately give your soloing ideas a more authentic sound without too much difficulty. Having said this, chromatics can sound random and aimless if used mindlessly!

In my book *Beginner Jazz Piano Soloing*, I introduced two simple chromatic passing note ideas. Let's recap these ideas over a ii – V – I sequence before moving on.

Descend Chromatically from Root To Seventh On Minor and Dominant 7 Chords

The first idea is simple but very effective.

Adding a chromatic passing note between the root and the 7th of a minor 7 or dominant 7 chord will give any phrase a much more interesting and authentic sound. Despite it being outside of the key, this chromatic note gives the phrase an exciting new element, as long as it has a definite direction and logic to it. You can see in this example how the chromatic passing note is added to a descending Dm7 arpeggio. Play it several times until you get used to the sound.

Example 1a

Now try this example using the chromatic passing note in a short two-bar lick.

Example 1b

As well as an arpeggio shape, you can embed that chromatic passing note into a scale-based line. Learn these two short ideas to understand how this works.

Example 1c

You can use the same idea over dominant 7 chords between the root and 7th in the same way.

Example 1d

Now let's try this concept in the context of a short lick as we did before.

Example 1e

Now, here are some more scalic ideas over the dominant 7.

Example 1f

Let's string these minor 7 and dominant 7 ideas together. Learn this line, which incorporates descending chromatic notes on Dm7 and G7 arpeggios. The chromatic passing notes are marked with a * so you can clearly see where they fall.

Example 1g

This next lick uses a more scale-based approach over the Dm7 chord.

Example 1h

Learn the above licks thoroughly and familiarise yourself with the sound of the chromatic passing notes. Only move on to the next idea when you're really comfortable with this first concept.

Chromatic Passing Notes Between Minor 3rds

Now we'll explore a slightly longer run and add chromatic passing notes between minor 3rd intervals. This approach involves identifying minor 3rd intervals between notes of the chord you are soloing over, then moving between them using chromatic passing notes.

Look at this Dm7 chord, where I've added brackets above the minor 3rd intervals. In a minor 7 chord there is a minor 3rd interval between the 5th and 7th, and between the root and 3rd.

Play this example many times to get comfortable with the concept.

Example 1i

Now try this lick over a Dm7 chord. I have marked the chromatic runs with brackets.

Example 1j

Let's examine how the same idea can be played on a dominant 7 chord. In this example, I will vary the direction and use both ascending and descending runs.

Example 1k

Try this lick over a G7 chord.

Example 1l

In a major 7 chord there is only one minor 3rd interval, which is between the 3rd and the 5th.

Example 1m

Try this short two-bar major 7 lick using a minor 3rd chromatic run.

Example 1n:

Now it's time to combine minor 3rd chromatic runs over a ii – V – I chord progression. Learn these two licks thoroughly and memorise them.

Example 1o

Example 1p

Chromatic Runs Between Major 3rd Intervals

Now let's move onto a new concept, which is one of my favourite chromatic techniques. Here we will extend the chromatic runs and use them on the bigger major 3rd intervals between chord tones. Chromatic runs between major 3rds can be incredibly effective and surprisingly easy once you grasp the concept. In a minor 7 chord there is a major 3rd distance between the 3rd and the 5th.

Example 1q

For dominant 7 chords, there is a major 3rd interval between the root and the 3rd.

Example 1r

In a major 7 chord, there are two major 3rd intervals: one between the root and the 3rd, and one between the 5th and the 7th.

Example 1s:

Major 3rd Chromatic Runs on Strong Beats

When playing in 1/8th notes, starting a major 3rd chromatic run on any beat means you'll land exactly two beats later. Starting on a strong beat, like beat one or three, will ensure you land two beats later on another strong beat, which makes the run sound natural and directional.

In Example 1t, notice that both major 3rd chromatic runs start on beat three of the bar and land naturally on beat one of the next bar. I've boxed the strong beats of the bar (one and three) so you can clearly see the effect.

Example 1t

Next, I've incorporated the same major 3rd chromatic runs as in Example 1t but added some surrounding notes to demonstrate how the idea can be integrated into a complete musical phrase.

Example 1u

This time I begin my major 3rd chromatic runs on the first beat of the bar so they neatly land on beat three. At the end of bar two, I've used a triplet arpeggio to transition into the second chromatic run. The combination of triplet arpeggios and chromatic runs is both idiomatic and effective.

Example 1v

Here's that triplet concept again.

Example 1w

You can also use the ascending form of the major 3rd chromatic run in a similar way.

Example 1x

Here's a reminder of the chromatic passing note methods we've used in this chapter:

1. To add a chromatic passing note when descending from the root to the 7th on minor and dominant 7 chords

2. To add chromatic passing notes between minor 3rd intervals

3. To add chromatic passing notes between major 3rd intervals

The three licks that follow combine all these concepts to make some lines that sound a bit more natural.

Example 1y

Example 1z

Example 1z1

Create Your Own Licks

Now it's time to think about writing some of your own licks using these chromatic techniques. Remember, when improperly used, chromatics can sound directionless and random, so be sure to aim for target notes that fall on strong beats and strive to sound purposeful and musical.

Revisit each concept in turn and see if you can invent some phrases you like. As you become more proficient, try combining concepts over a ii – V – I progression.

Longer Exercise

To conclude this chapter, I want you to learn a short piece to more fully grasp how chromatic passing notes can be used in an actual melody. This example contains the chromatic ideas we have studied in this chapter – ideas you can use in your solos.

Example 1z2

10 G7 Cmaj7 3 3 Dm7
14 G7 Cmaj7 E7
19 A7 D7 G7
24 Dm7 G7 Cmaj7 3 3
29 Dm7 G7 Cmaj7 Dm7
34 G7 Cmaj7 3 3

Once you have mastered this piece, play along to the backing track. Enjoy the experience of just jamming over the track and using chromatic ideas to enrich your solo.

Chapter Two: Left Hand Chords

Your left hand is important in jazz soloing because it provides the harmonic context for your solos. It fulfils the roles of laying down accompanying chords and punctuating your licks with rhythmic chord stabs; it creates the possibility of counter melodies, and can provide accompanying basslines when needed.

In this chapter we'll focus on its chordal role and learn how to streamline chords to make them more elegant and easier to play.

If you worked through my beginner book, you'll have used four-note 7th chords and reconfigured their shapes to make changing between chords more efficient. However, these basic four-note chords can feel and sound quite cumbersome when you're soloing. The solution is to streamline them by omitting some of the less important notes. But the question is, which notes can we lose?

Streamlining a Cmaj7 Chord

Let's examine a Cmaj7 chord and identify the notes that are most important.

The Root

You might assume that the root is essential, but if you're playing in a band with a bass player, this note will already be covered, so we can omit the root. Chords without the root are often referred to simply as *rootless chords* or *rootless voicings*. Omitting the root also has the added benefit of freeing up a finger to add more colourful notes to the chord.

The 3rd

The 3rd of the chord is crucial because it determines whether it is major or minor, so we need to retain the 3rd. Because the 3rd dictates the *quality* of the chord, we refer to it as a *guide tone*.

The 5th

The 5th of the chord doesn't define it in any significant way. It remains consistent whether the chord is major or minor, so we can exclude it.

The 7th

The 7th is vital because, without it, the chord ceases to be a 7th chord. It also determines the type of 7th chord – whether it's a major, minor, or dominant 7. The 7th is also a guide tone, so we must keep it.

Example 2a

Cmaj7

Cmaj7 without
the root note.

Cmaj7 without
the root or the fifth.

The third and
the seventh are
the 'guide tones'.

When we extract the guide tones, it's like playing the essence of the chord. By using just two notes we can streamline the left-hand part to make it much easier to play and more pleasing to the ear. This example shows how guide tones can be used to move through a ii – V – I chord progression.

Example 2b

Dm7   G7   Cmaj7

Full Dm7   Dm7 guide   Full G7   G7 guide   Full Cmaj7   Cmaj7 guide
chord   tones   chord   tones   chord   tones

Inverting the guide tones on some of the chords enables your left hand to exercise extreme economy of movement.

In the next example I have inverted the 3rd and 7th (F and B) of the G7 chord, which allows minimal movement between chords. In fact, moving from Dm7 to G7 requires changing just one note by a half-step as the C moves down to a B.

Moving from G7 to Cmaj7 also requires only a single half-step movement as the F descends to the E.

Example 2c

Dm⁷   G⁷   Here on the G7 I have inverted
the third (B).   Cmaj7

2

Here is the 2 5 1 progression with just guide tones. The G7 guide tones are inverted. Note how minimal the movement is between each chord.

Dm⁷   G⁷   Cmaj7

You can also invert the entire ii – V – I progression so that it sounds a bit lower down on the keyboard.

Example 2d

Dm⁷   G⁷   Cmaj7

2

Here are the same chords as above but with the upper guide tone taken down an octave

Dm⁷   G⁷   Cmaj7

Getting familiar with guide tones is an essential task for any jazz pianist. When you know the guide tones well, navigating jazz chord sequences becomes much easier. Your brain can instantly construct playable and authentic accompaniments for your solos. Additionally, you'll be able to mentally track the important notes of the chords and incorporate them into your right-hand lines.

When you are accustomed to guide tones it's also easy to add more exotic notes to your chords, as you are now only using two fingers for each voicing.

Guide Tones Through All the Keys

For practice, we'll play ii – V – I progressions in all keys using just guide tones. Below are examples in various keys.

F Major

Example 2e

G Major

Example 2f

Bb Major

Example 2g

Eb Major

Example 2h

Ab Major

Example 2i

Db Major

Example 2j

Ebm⁷   Ab⁷   Dbmaj7

D Major

Example 2k

Em⁷   A⁷   Dmaj7

A Major

Example 2l

Bm⁷   E⁷   Amaj7

E Major

Example 2m

B Major

Example 2n

F#/Gb Major

Example 2o

By practicing these guide tones in different keys, you'll improve your ability to adapt quickly and effortlessly to any key during a performance.

The next step is to combine these ii – V – I progressions into a longer chord sequence. Here are two examples that guide you through all the keys. Your goal is to play through both examples fluently with the backing track.

Example 2p

27

Example 2q

Lastly, test yourself and see if you can work out the guide tones for the chord chart below. Grab some manuscript paper and jot them down.

Example 2r

|: Dm7	G7	CMaj7	
Gm7	C7	FMaj7	
F#m7	B7	Em7	A7
Dm7	G7	CMaj7	:|
Bm7	E7	AMaj7	
Am7	D7	GMaj7	
|: Gm7	C7	FMaj7	
F#m7	B7	Em7	A7
Dm7	G7	CMaj7	:|

As you become more confident with guide tone voicings, try playing them while adding the right-hand licks you learned in the previous chapter.

We'll continue using guide tones throughout the rest of this book, which will help you become more familiar with them.

Chapter Three: Chord Extensions

Chord extensions are used extensively in modern jazz and are integral to its style as they add richness and subtle tensions to the harmony. Without them the modern jazz sound wouldn't exist. In this chapter, we'll explore some of the more commonly used extensions, both in block chords and melodic lines.

Chord extensions are notes that are played more than an octave above the root note. For instance, to add a 9th to a Dm7 chord, we count up nine notes from the root and find that E is the 9th of Dm7 (see table below).

Interval	1	2	3	4	5	6	7	8	9	10	11	12	13	14	1
D Dorian Scale	D	E	F	G	A	B	C	D	E	F	G	A	B	C	D

The 9th

The 9th creates a beautiful harmony over both major and minor chords. In this example, you can see how we locate the 9th on a Dm7 chord by counting up the notes from the root.

Example 3a

Now we'll find the 9th on a Cmaj7 chord.

Example 3b

Three Licks Using 9ths

These licks explore the sound of the 9th interval over Dm7 and Cmaj7 chords. I've highlighted the 9ths with a *.

Example 3c

The next line shows how playing the 9th creates an Fmaj7 arpeggio over the Dm7 chord and an Em7 arpeggio over the Cmaj7 chord.

Example 3d

Here, I've resolved the phrase onto the root of Dm7, rounding it off nicely. On the Cmaj7 chord, I ended the phrase on the 9th. Staying on the 9th at the end of a phrase creates an open feeling that's less anchored to the harmony.

Example 3e

The 11th

The 11th works well over minor 7 chords but some caution is needed over major 7 chords. Here's how to find the 11th on a minor 7 chord.

Example 3f

Here you can see two Cmaj7 chords with an added 11th. The first chord includes a natural 11th (F), and you'll hear it doesn't sound great.

The F creates a clash with the E in the lower part of the chord and, although dissonances are often embraced in jazz, this particular one is normally undesirable.

For this reason, we typically raise the 11th by a semi-tone on major 7 chords and play a major 7#11, as I have done in the second Cmaj7 chord by adding an F#.

When we raise the 11th on a chord we call it the *sharp eleventh* or just *sharp eleven* (#11). This note can sound quite exotic if you're not used to it, but it is much preferable on major chords.

Example 3g

Sharp
11th

Sharp
11th

Root 1   2nd   3rd   4th   5th   6th   7th   Octave 8th   9th   10th

Cmaj7

Three Licks Using the Eleventh

Here is a lick using the 11th on a Dm7 chord and again over a Cmaj7 chord. I've marked all the 11ths with a *.

Example 3h

Dm7

5   Cmaj7

When the 11th is combined with the 9th and the 7th (G, E and C respectively on Dm7) this creates a C major arpeggio over the Dm7 harmony.

On the Cmaj7 chord, a B minor arpeggio (F#, D and B) is made in the same way.

Example 3i

Now we'll throw in the 5th with the 7th, 9th and 11th. This creates a whole Am7 arpeggio over the Dm7 chord and a Gmaj7 arpeggio over the Cmaj7 chord.

Example 3j

The 13th

The next extension we'll explore is the 13th. Just like the other extensions, you can locate the 13th by counting up from the root note.

Example 3k

Three Licks Using the 13th

Below are some licks to help you become familiar with using the 13th. As before, I've marked the 13th with a *.

Example 3l

In this next example, try to identify some 11ths as well as the 13ths.

Example 3m

The following lick incorporates a few 9ths, along with 11ths and 13ths. See if you can spot all these extensions. These three extensions form a triad which you can superimpose over the harmony. Here, I've marked an E minor triad over the Dm7 chord, and a D major triad over the Cmaj7 chord.

Example 3n

When we add the 13th on top of the 9th and 11th, we create a whole new chord shape composed entirely of extensions which can be superimposed over the original chord.

In this example I've stacked a 9th (E), an 11th (G), and a 13th (B) over the Dm7 chord in the left hand. The three extension notes of E, G, and B form an E minor chord.

The second chord is a Cmaj7 chord with a 9th, a #11, and a 13th (D, F#, and A) stacked above it. These extension notes create a D major triad over the Cmaj7 chord.

Example 3o

Five Licks Exploring 9ths, 11ths and 13ths over Dm7 and Cmaj7 chords

These three extensions are the most commonly used in jazz, so it's essential to familiarise yourself thoroughly with them.

I've written two versions of each lick – one over a Dm7 chord and a second over a Cmaj7 chord – allowing you to experience the characteristics of each extension over both major and minor chords. The first idea uses all the extensions along with the 7th.

As noted previously, using the 13th with the 11th and 9th allows us to "think" of soloing with an E minor triad over the Dm7, and a D major triad over the Cmaj7.

If we also add the 7th, it's like superimposing a whole Cmaj7 arpeggio over the Dm7 chord and a Bm7 arpeggio over the Cmaj7 chord.

Example 3p

Let's explore more possibilities of arpeggio shapes that we can superimpose over chords to add extensions. Try to identify which arpeggios and extensions are being used.

Example 3q

In Example 3r, we delve further into the possibilities for arpeggio shapes. Pay attention to the series of triad shapes being used here.

Example 3r

Create Your Own Licks

Now it's time for you to write some of your own licks that explore the 9th, 11th, and 13th extensions. Start by using the Dm7 and Cmaj7 chords, but then challenge yourself to transpose them to other minor and major 7 chords. Aim to make your licks musical and playable, so that they can become an integral part of your growing jazz vocabulary.

Longer Exercise

Finally, here's a piece for you to learn that combines all the concepts in this chapter. Pay close attention to the chord extensions used in the melody and the solo. Once you have learned the piece, play it along with the backing track.

Learn the written solo, then try improvising your own. Use the licks that you've composed in this chapter and mix and match the ideas you've learned so far to create varied solos. As you gain confidence, challenge yourself to come up with some spontaneously improvised ideas as well.

Example 3s

Dm7
Cmaj7
Dm7
6
Cmaj7
Dm7
Solo
Cmaj7
12
Dm7
Cmaj7
17
Dm7
Cmaj7
Dm7
22
Cmaj7
Dm7
Head
27
Cmaj7
Dm7
Cmaj7

Chapter Four: Altering the 9th

Now we have a working knowledge of extensions we can start using them in more interesting ways to create the bebop vocabulary that is central to the language of modern jazz.

In the early 1940s, alto saxophonist Charlie Parker was a pivotal figure in a new jazz movement that became known as bebop. He once said, "I realised by using the high notes of the chords as a melodic line, and by the right harmonic progression, I could play what I heard inside me. That's when I was born."

By "the high notes" Parker was referring to the chord extensions of the 9th, 11th and 13th. However, a large part of his playing was to alter these extensions to add additional tensions into his melodic lines.

Altering an extension means to sharpen or flatten the interval. This is most commonly done on dominant 7 chords, which typically appear as the V7 chord in a II – V – I progression. Altering extended notes on the V chord adds much more tension to the harmony or melody, before the resolution "home" occurs on chord I. These altered extensions can create some pretty tense sounds, especially when used in combinations.

Listen to as much Charlie Parker, Dizzy Gillespie and Bud Powell as you can to hear the bebop language spoken by the greats. Now, let's look at the most common alterations.

The b9

One of the most commonly used alterations in bebop is the b9, which is often added to dominant 7 chords. Let's introduce it into your soloing language in a couple of practical ways.

Melodic Movement

Within a ii – V – I chord progression, playing the b9 on the V7 chord can create a strong chromatic line:

- Play the fifth of the Dm7 chord (A)

- Descend to the b9 of the G7 chord to play the note Ab

- Finally, resolve this tension to the 5th of the Cmaj7 chord (G)

This is now a descending melody that moves in chromatic steps.

Example 4a

Target Notes

We already know that using chromatic movement in our soloing is an effective way to create a strong sense of direction. Let's explore this further and use the previous A to Ab to G notes as targets in our solo line. Although the following ideas contains other notes, it's these target notes that we will emphasise in the melodic line.

It's crucial to place these target notes on strong beats (one or three). This ensures that they will coincide with important beats to make the chromatic movement clear to the listener.

Below are some licks that use this chromatic movement as their foundation. I've highlighted the A, Ab, and G movement, and they land on beats one and three each time.

This idea contains two small licks. I've halved the length of the chords so that the Dm7 and G7 occupy only two beats each. This allows us to see the chromatic movement more obviously.

Example 4b

Let's return to four beat chords where we place those descending chromatic notes of A, Ab, and G on beat one of each bar.

The idea is to focus on playing the chromatic notes on the first beat of each bar, then fitting other notes around them. The strength of the sequence is so compelling that you can play nearly anything in between without losing musical coherence.

Example 4c

Example 4d

Example 4e

Forming a Diminished Structure

Another way to use the b9 is to create a *diminished* structure. Diminished chords are built from four notes a minor 3rd apart and create a tense sound.

Example 4f

Here's how we can use the b9 to create that diminished tension within a lick. Taking G7 as an example, the chord tones are G, B, D, and F (the root, 3rd, 5th and 7th).

If we replace the G with Ab (the b9), we have Ab, B, D, and F. This set of notes, with Ab replacing G, forms an Abdim7 arpeggio and is what you played in the previous example.

So, if we replace the root of the dominant chord (G7) with the b9 (Ab), we create an Ab diminished arpeggio, and when we play it over a G bass note we create a G7b9 chord.

Example 4g

Below are some licks that highlight this diminished sound. Notice that you don't really hear the dark effect of the diminished chord as you did in Example 4f, even though you're playing the same notes. As you're playing it over the G7 chord you only really hear it as a G7b9 sound. I've highlighted the diminished arpeggio shapes with a bracket.

Example 4h

Now for some longer licks using the b9 to create diminished arpeggio shapes.

Example 4i

Example 4j

Example 4k

The #9

The #9 is another common, distinctive sound in jazz. It's important to know that the #9 creates a strong dissonance, as it is only a semitone away from the major third of the chord. Try playing B and an A# together and you'll hear this tension. However, when the same notes are placed in a G7 chord they blend beautifully. This dissonance characterises the #9 sound.

Example 4l

Here are some licks to familiarise you with the #9 sound. I've marked each #9 with a *.

Example 4m

Example 4n

Example 4o

In bebop soloing, the #9 is often used alongside the b9 and it's time to become comfortable using both. These licks incorporate both the #9 and b9.

Example 4p

Example 4q

Example 4r

Example 4s

Create Your Own Licks

Now try writing some of your own licks that use #9 and b9 tensions.

Longer Exercise

Here is a piece written in the style of some great bebop legends. I have included chromatic passing notes, b9s, and #9s in both the melody and the solo. Once you've mastered all the licks in this chapter, have a go at playing your own solo using b9 and #9 notes.

Example 4t

18
Cmaj7
Am7
Dm7
G7
Cmaj7
Am7
Dm7
G7
22
Gm7
C7
Fmaj7
B♭7
Dm7
G7
Cmaj7
D.S al Fine

Chapter Five: Altering the 13th

It's impossible to achieve an authentic bebop sound without using the 13th in both its natural and flattened forms. The natural 13th pairs beautifully with the b9, and the b13 is extensively used in bebop solos on dominant 7 chords.

The Natural 13 With the b9

Although this chapter focuses on altering the 13th, I want to introduce you to the combination of the natural 13th with the b9 because of its beauty. Using natural extensions alongside altered extensions in the same phrase can produce some exquisite sounds, particularly the combination of the 13th with the b9.

Taking the II – V – I progression, over the G7 chord the natural 13th is an E, and the b9 is an Ab. Below are some licks that utilise this combination, and I've marked the natural 13ths with an *.

Example 5a

Example 5b

Example 5c

Example 5d

The b13

Now let's explore the b13. Adding this note creates an augmented sound because the b13 is the same note as the augmented 5th (5+). For example, the b13 of G is Eb, and the +5 is D#, which are the same notes. Although I will say b13 throughout, thinking of this note a +5 can be helpful.

You can see this equivalence in the next example. Note that we omit the 5th (D) from the G7b13 chord as it clashes with the b13 (Ab).

Example 5e

Here are some licks that highlight the G7b13 sound.

Example 5f

Example 5g

Example 5h

b13 Licks on G7 from Ab Minor Structures

Another interesting soloing approach on a G7 chord is to play an Ab minor triad, as it contains both the b13 and b9 along with the 3rd of the dominant 7 chord. The notes in Ab minor are Ab, Cb (B), and Eb.

To use this concept, simply think of playing the minor chord a semitone above the dominant chord you are soloing over. In this case, Abm over G7.

Example 5i

Abm   G7(♭13 ♭9)

This is an Ab minor chord spelt correctly with an Ab, Cb and Eb.

Here is the same chord with the middle note spelt B rather than a Cb

Using the flat thirteen (Eb), the flat nine (Ab) and the third (B), we can construct an Ab minor Arpeggio over a G7 chord

Let's explore some b13 licks that are built around Ab minor structures.

Example 5j

Dm7   G7   Cmaj7

Ab minor arpeggio

Example 5k

Dm7   G7   Ab minor arpeggio   Cmaj7

Example 5l

Exploring b13 Licks

The next example shows two different ways to approach the b13 melodically on some "quick" changes. In the first phrase, a descending chromatic run targets the b13. The second ascends an arpeggio up to the 9th of Dm7 (E), which then drops to the b13 on the G7.

Example 5m

See if you can identify any other altered extensions used alongside the b13 in these licks.

Example 5n

Example 5o

Example 5p

The previous licks all worked over a major II – V – I progression, but what about other chord sequences?

A common approach among jazz musicians is to learn solos by heart, to internalise the language of the musicians that inspire us. This often involves listening carefully to each phrase over and over again, copying it, writing it down, and gradually bringing it into your own solos, before varying it so that it becomes your own. It requires patience and a bit of obsession, but the effort is well worth it.

Here is a solo written using the bebop concepts we've covered so far. Try to learn it by ear from the recording rather than just reading the music, and ensure that you memorise the entire piece.

See if you can recognise elements we've discussed, such as chromatic passing notes, flat/natural 9ths, and flat/natural 13ths.

Example 5q

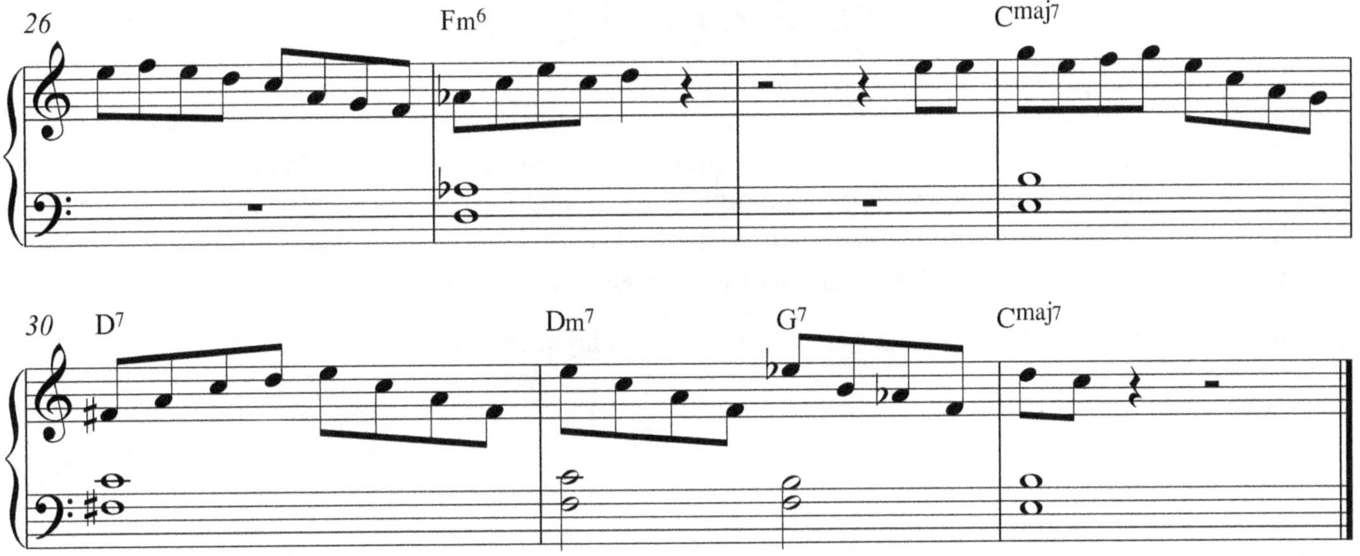
26
Fm6
Cmaj7
30
D7
Dm7
G7
Cmaj7

Chapter Six: Altering the 11th

Adding the 11th to your palette will complete the list of extensions needed for your bebop vocabulary. As mentioned earlier, the 11th fits comfortably on minor 7 chords but not as well on major 7 and dominant 7 chords. To improve the sound of the 11th on dominant and major 7 chords, we sharpen it. While alterations to extensions usually increase dissonance, sharpening the 11th on chords with a major 3rd is an exception, as it actually reduces dissonance by avoiding a semitone clash with the 3rd.

Listen again to the sound the 11th and #11th create as you play these chords:

Example 6a

While this altered note is always referred to as a #11, it is sometimes easier to write it as a b5 depending on the key signature. Here are some licks that demonstrate how you might use the #11 in a solo:

Example 6b

On the G7 chord below, notice how the #11 (C#) combines with the 9th (A) and the 13th (E) to form an A major arpeggio.

Example 6c

Now see how the #11th is used to create a different major arpeggio. Over the G7, the #11 (spelled Db instead of C#) forms a Db major arpeggio (Db, F, Ab) when combined with the b9 and 7th (F).

Example 6d

Adding the #11 to our collection of altered extensions gives us all the notes needed to complete two useful scales: The Altered scale, and the Half-Whole Diminished scale. Both scales work beautifully over the V7 chord in a II – V – I chord progression.

Exploring the Half-Whole Scale

First, let's delve into the Half-Whole scale, sometimes known as the Dominant Diminished scale. The reason for this name becomes clear when you examine the pattern of intervals that form the steps of the scale.

The Half-Whole scale is an eight-note synthetic scale that is created by arranging the notes with a half-step (semitone) between the first two notes, and a whole step (tone) between the next two. This pattern repeats throughout the scale as you can see below:

H W H W H W H W

The scale formula (interval pattern) is shown below, and I've written it starting on a G. As you can see, it includes all the arpeggio notes of a G7 chord along with the extensions b9, #9, #11 and 13.

G Half-Whole	G	Ab	A#	B	C#	D	E	F
Intervals	1	b9	#9	3	#11	5	13	7

You can also, view this scale as the combination of two diminished arpeggios: G diminished (G, Bb/A/#, Db/C#, and E) and Ab diminished (Ab, B, D, and F) which you saw before in the earlier b9 section. These two diminished arpeggios combined give us all the notes needed for the G Half-Whole scale.

Play through the next example to get used to the sound of this scale.

Example 6e

Half tone/Whole tone scale

Example 6f

Here are some licks which use the Half-Whole scale.

Example 6g

Example 6h

The Altered Scale

The Altered scale is named due to it containing every altered extension, making it perfect for some "out-there" dissonance on dominant 7 chords. Unlike the Half-Whole scale, which contains the natural 13th, the Altered scale flattens the 13th.

It starts with an identical pattern of intervals as the Half-Whole scale, but transitions into a series of whole tones from the 3rd. Notice that the altered scale does not contain a natural 5th, which can make it sound a bit unstable if you don't use it well.

G Altered	G	Ab	A#	B	C#	Eb	F
Intervals	1	b9	#9	3	#11 / b5	b13 / +5	7

Example 6i

Altered scale

You can also see the Altered scale as having the same notes as the melodic minor scale starting from a semitone above the chord.

Example 6j

Applying the Altered Scale

Now, let's put theory into practice with some licks that use the G Altered scale.

Example 6k

Example 6l

Example 6m

This solo study incorporates all the concepts we've discussed so far. I've annotated the solo to help you understand what is happening at each point, and a brief analysis follows on from it.

Example 6n

Sharp 11th

These notes
are the same
as an E Major
arpeggio.

Chromatic
movement
interspersed
with other notes

Sharp 11th

Solo Analysis

Over the G7 in bar two, we see the use of the b9 (Ab) and the #11 (spelt Db here). These altered extensions combine to form a Db arpeggio shape.

In bar six, note the use of the b13 (Eb) along with both #9 and b9 tensions (Bb and Ab) over the G7 chord. This bar utilises most of the notes in the G Altered scale, demonstrating a rich use of extensions.

By bar ten, almost all the notes of the altered scale are in play, specifically the B Altered scale over B7. Bar twelve continues with altered extensions but introduces a varied rhythm, starting with a 1/4 note followed by triplets on beat three, breaking the continuity of the 1/8th notes.

In bar fourteen, the #11 over the G7 chord (notated as Db in the score) is prominent and appears twice. Initially, it combines with the b9, with the Db descending a 4th to Ab, creating a distinct, jagged sound. The second appearance is the start of an altered scale run.

The repeated C at the start of bar seventeen is echoed at the beginning of bar eighteen, but raised a semi-tone to Db, the #11 of the G7 chord.

Bar twenty-two features a harmonious blend of a natural 13th (E) and a b9 (Ab), forming an E major arpeggio shape (spelled with an Ab instead of a G#), superbly layered over the G7 harmony.

Bars twenty-three and twenty-four introduce short sequences of chromatic passing 1/16th notes that add some rhythmic diversity.

Bars twenty-five to twenty-six see an F# Minor scale transform into a B Altered scale, showcasing a fluid transition between scales.

Bars 27-28 present a sleek chromatic movement from D# to D natural, concluding on C#, the 3rd of A7, interspersed with additional notes for texture.

Bar thirty rounds out the section by incorporating most of the altered extensions into an arpeggio-like figure, culminating in the distinctive #11.

Chapter Seven: The Minor 7b5 Chord

The minor 7b5 is an essential chord to master. As the name implies, it is similar to the minor 7 chord but contains a flattened fifth (b5). It is also known as a half-diminished chord because, unlike a fully diminished chord where intervals are all stacked minor thirds, here the root, 3rd, and 5th are a minor third apart creating a diminished triad, but the 7th is a major 3rd from the 5th, disrupting the diminished interval pattern.

Example 7a

The Minor ii – V – i

The m7b5 chord is most commonly played as the II chord in a minor ii – V – i progression. Minor ii – V – i progressions are common in jazz standards and essential know. The minor ii – V – i works in a similar way to its major counterpart but with slight changes in the chord qualities to suit minor keys.

Let's compare the chords in the major and minor ii – V – i.

Example 7b

- The I chord (C) is a major 7 in the major progression and minor 7 in the minor progression

- The V chord (G7) remains consistent across both major and minor progressions

- The II chord is the most notable difference. In the minor ii – V – i it is a m7b5

Guide Tone Version

The guide tone version of the minor II – V – I closely resembles the major version. Notice in the next example that the primary difference lies in the flattening of the notes on chord I.

Example 7c

Remember, guide tones consist solely of the 3rd and 7th of a chord and omit the 5th. This means that when you play a minor ii – V – i using just guide tones, you will exclude the b5 of the II chord. Notice in the example above that there is no Ab included in the Dm7b5 chord.

Therefore, to clearly distinguish it from regular minor 7 chords, it is beneficial to add the b5 to the II chord like this:

Example 7d

The m7b5 Chord in a Minor ii - V - i

We flatten the 5th of the ii chord because this is the correct note in the minor scale. For example, the Dm7b5 chord includes a b5 (Ab) because Ab is a note found in the tonic key of C Minor.

Example 7e

The A flat is necessary due to being in the key of C minor.

Adding a 9th to the m7b5

So far, so good, but things become more interesting when we consider adding a 9th. If I want to add a 9th to the Dm7b5 chord, the key of C Minor suggests that this note should be an Eb.

However, when I play an Eb over the Dm7b5 chord, it sounds quite dissonant against the root note (D). A common choice among jazz musicians is to use the natural 9th (E). This might seem counterintuitive because E natural is not typically found in the key of C Minor, yet it does produce a more pleasing sound.

Example 7f

Using the natural 9th on the m7b5 influences our note selection when soloing. With the inclusion of the natural 9th, the selection of notes over a Dm7b5 chord becomes as follows.

Example 7g

The natural 9th also enriches the melodic journey your licks can go on. For instance, in the key of C Minor, using E natural over the ii chord before resolving to Eb on the V or I chord, creates a compelling effect. The E natural introduces a slight tension (as you're playing the major 3rd, E, in a minor key), which resolves beautifully to Eb, bringing the sound harmoniously home.

Try these licks to see how it works:

Example 7h

Example 7i

Example 7j

Minor ii V i Licks in Different Keys

Here are some more minor II – V – I licks that explore various keys:

Minor ii – V – i in A Minor.

Example 7k

Minor ii – V – i in D Minor.

Note the 9th of the Em7b5 appears as an F# in the right-hand line in bar one.

Example 7l

Minor ii – V – i in G Minor.

Example 7m

Minor ii – V – i in F Minor.

Example 7n

Minor ii – V – i in E Minor.

Example 7o

Finally, here is a solo that's rich in minor ii – V – i sequences. Master it thoroughly, then try out some of your own ideas along with the backing track.

Example 7p

Chapter Eight: Introducing Modes

When you add the 9th, 11th, and 13th between the chord tones (root, 3rd, 5th, and 7th), you build a complete scale.

Figure 1.

Thinking of notes as either extensions or chord tones is useful because it contextualizes them in relation to a chord and helps us to choose appropriate notes when the chords are moving quickly. But there is another way to think about note choice when the chords are more static.

When a piece of music spends a long time on one chord – for example, eight or sixteen bars – we can change our thinking and view each chord as having its own scale or *mode* that we can use to improvise in a less arpeggio-based way.

Understanding both approaches is important because our thought processes influence our playing, and different ways of thinking about chords and scales provide fresh perspectives and inspiration.

For instance, musicians who primarily think in terms of scales often play in a scalic manner. This often sounds melodic but can result in their solos sounding too scalic and boring.

Conversely, those who focus on chord tones and extensions typically play a lot of arpeggios. These melodies contain strong melodic leaps and can create more interest. However, those players can become too reliant on chord structures and struggle to create ideas when limited to a single chord.

Alternating between these ways of thinking within a solo can spark new ideas and open up different musical possibilities. So, in this chapter, we'll begin to explore the *modal* approach to soloing.

Modal Jazz

When you hear the term *modal jazz*, it refers to music that focuses on playing for extended periods over a single chord, allowing the musician to explore the possibilities of one scale or *mode* for a more extended period. A prime example of this style is the track *So What* by Miles Davis. This track is essential listening for all jazz musicians because it was one of the first jazz tunes to use long periods of static harmony. It's formed from sixteen bars of Dm7, eight bars of Ebm7, and finishes with another eight bars of Dm7 – quite different from the fast, challenging key changes of the bop period.

Staying on one chord for a long period enables you to think in a more linear manner, and you don't need to worry about adjusting notes to accommodate chord changes. For instance, if you are playing over a Dm7 chord without any changes, you can rely solely on the notes of its parent scale without finding any discordant notes.

In fact, one of the main characteristics of modal soloing is that *all* the notes of the scale are given equal importance. Yes, the root, b3, 5th and b7 of the Dm7 will be slightly stronger chord tones, but a soloist will be able to sit for longer on the 9th, 11th and 13th of the scale.

What is a Mode?

A mode is created by playing the notes of a scale from a different starting point. We know that the C Major scale contains the notes: C D E F G A B C. If we play those notes beginning on the D note, we have in fact created a mode (called the Dorian mode).

The Dorian mode is considered a scale in its own right, because it has a different formula from the major scale.

In the C Major scale, the distance from C to D is a tone, and from D to E is a tone. If we continue this process we get:

Tone Tone Semitone Tone Tone Tone Semitone

We can describe this pattern in intervals, so that we assign the major scale the very simple formula of:

1 2 3 4 5 6 7

This formula *defines* the major scale. Any changes to this structure change it from being a major scale.

When we play the notes of C Major starting on D, we get, D E F G A B C, and a new formula of 1 2 b3 4 5 6 b7, because the intervals are now different relative to the root note.

The first interval from D to E is a tone. That's the same as the major scale.

But the distance from E to F is a semitone, which is very different from the major scale. This new scale has a minor 3rd interval between its first and third notes – the defining characteristic of a minor scale.

The Dorian mode is perfect for playing over long stretches of minor 7 chords. However, because it contains the natural 6th of the major scale (as opposed to the b6 of the natural minor or melodic minor scales), it doesn't sound as "dark".

Seven modes can be constructed from the major scale using this method, but the most useful to us as jazz musicians at this stage are the Dorian, Mixolydian and Lydian. The table below shows the formulas for these modes compared to the major scale (also known as the Ionian mode).

Mode Name	Formula						
Major / Ionian	1	2	3	4	5	6	7
Dorian	1	2	min3	4	5	6	min7
Lydian	1	2	3	aug4	5	6	7
Mixolydian	1	2	3	4	5	6	min7

Dorian, Mixolydian and Lydian are the most common scales used in modal jazz. Take a moment to play them over their appropriate chords in the following three examples.

Example 8a

Example 8b

Example 8c

The Dorian mode is suitable for minor 7 chords, Mixolydian is used over dominant 7s, and Lydian offers an intriguing choice for major 7 chords. To give you a brief flavour of these sounds, here are some licks using these three modes.

Three Dorian Licks

These licks are played over a full Dm7 chord to help you lock into that Dorian sound.

Example 8d

Example 8e

Example 8f

Three Mixolydian Licks

In these examples, the left hand grounds the harmony with a low 5th. This approach fits well with the modal strategies we'll explore later in this book.

Example 8g

Example 8h

Example 8i

Three Lydian Licks

These C Lydian licks are played over a full Cmaj7 chord to help you hear the notes in context. Try a Cmaj7#11 chord too if you want to really hear the Lydian (1 2 3 #4 5 6 7) in action!

Example 8j

Example 8k

Example 8l

Write Your Own Licks

Now it's time for you to write two licks for each of these modes. I've chosen modes based on all the white notes to simplify your thinking melodically, so you don't have to worry about any sharps or flats.

- Write two D Dorian licks over a Dm7 chord

- Write two G Mixolydian licks over a G7 chord

- Write two F Lydian licks over an Fmaj7 chord

Learn a Tune

The following tune is built around long periods spent on a single chord, which allows you to explore the sounds of the Dorian mode over a Dm7 chord, and the Lydian mode over a Cmaj7 chord.

Notice the use of arpeggio shapes in the solo, such as superimposing an E minor triad over the Dm7 harmony (the notes E, G, and B, respectively the 9th, 11th and 13th). Also notice the scalic passages in the solo, such as bars 26-27.

When you've learned the tune, play the licks you've learned in the solo section then mix them up to create new ideas, and attempt to invent some spontaneous licks as well. Use the D Dorian mode over the Dm7 chord and C Lydian over the Cmaj7 chord.

Example 8m

Chapter Nine: Melodic Soloing on Modal Jazz

There are two important and complementary approaches to modal playing that you should know:

1. The melodic approach

2. The pentatonic/pattern-based approach.

You can use both approaches to become a more versatile soloist.

The Melodic Approach

As we've touched upon, the intention behind Miles' *Kind of Blue* album was to move away from the increasingly complex harmonies of bebop/hard bop and return to simpler, more accessible forms of harmony that allowed for more freedom of expression. He felt that the jazz tunes of the time were becoming crowded with difficult chord changes, and the burden of negotiating this harmony was beginning to stifle creativity.

Davis was attracted to the modal approach proposed by musicians such as George Russell, as a way of creating space, allowing improvisers to think more melodically, and express themselves with more freedom. On *Kind of Blue*, you can hear Miles using space and melodic ideas to great effect. It's almost as if you can hear him exclaiming, "Look at all this space – I can breathe again!"

This melodic, spacious style is intrinsically linked to the modal style and is something we can use effectively in our own playing

Play What's in Your Head and Unleash Your Imagination

The melodic modal soloing style is an excellent gateway for developing the skill of playing what you hear in your head. It simplifies the process of improvisation by removing the requirement to juggle complex chords. Instead, you can focus solely on imagining beautiful melodies and reproducing them on your instrument. In fact, being able to play what you hear in your mind is the ultimate goal for all your soloing.

In this section, I'm not going to offer you numerous licks and phrases. Instead, you'll learn some powerful exercises to help develop your ability to spontaneously imagine and play ideas on the piano.

Exercise One – Sing the Sounds

The first exercise involves familiarising yourself with the sound of each note in the mode. We'll use D Dorian here, but I encourage you to apply the same process to the Lydian and Mixolydian modes too.

Play each note of the Dorian mode slowly, letting the notes resonate, and sing each note just after you've played it. Each note has its own distinct character within the context of the mode. To help you think about and internalise every note, you could compose a sentence or two about the character of each note. Here are some of my thoughts, but you should try to think of your own descriptions of the way the notes make you feel when sustained over a Dm7 chord.

Note one (D): This note feels like the home base. It's the root of the Dm7 chord and the tonal centre of the mode. It's safe note, ideal for concluding a phrase.

Note two (E): This note is the first departure point in the scale, serving as a useful connecting or passing note between the root and 3rd. However, it sounds beautifully detached from the minor 7 chord when used as a 9th, especially in combination with other extensions.

Note three (F): As the minor 3rd, this note gives the Dorian mode its minor quality. It's the 3rd of the Dm7 chord and therefore a "safe" note to finish a phrase on.

Note four (G): This fourth note serves as a connecting or passing note between the 3rd and 5th. As the 11th, it fits beautifully over minor chords and pairs well with other extensions, sounding detached yet harmonious.

Note five (A): An important note in Western harmony, and in a modal context it doesn't "challenge" the character of the chord. It is the dominant note of the chord and offers a slight tension before returning to the tonic.

Note six (B): This natural 6th distinguishes the Dorian mode from the natural minor scale. The natural 6th on a minor chord adds a glimmer of hope in an otherwise minor tonality.

Note seven (C): This note does challenge our Western classical harmonic expectations. In D Melodic Minor, you'd expect a raised 7th following a raised 6th, but the b7 change to min7 in Dorian brings a slightly bluesy, relaxed feel to the minor chord.

Now you try! Try to describe the character and sound of each note as you play and sing it over a Dm7 chord. There are no wrong answers. You might feel like describing a note as happy, sad, yellow, pungent, tight, dreamy, or menacing. There are no rules, it's all about you finding ways to relate feelings to the notes in your music.

Next, play the whole mode a bit faster and sing it back. Consider recording yourself to check your accuracy. Repeat this as often as you need until you are confident that you can sing it from memory.

Finally, sing the mode first and *then* play it on the piano. Recording yourself and listening back can help ensure you've captured it accurately.

When you're ready, repeat these steps with Lydian and Mixolydian

Example 9a

Dorian on D

Exercise Two – Sing and Play Some Notes

This exercise will help connect your body and mind to the Dorian mode. Start by playing and singing a D note and choose, but don't play, another note to sing after it.

Now, play the D on the piano again, then sing your chosen second note without playing it. Just imagine playing it on the piano as you sing it.

After singing, try playing the two notes on the piano to check if you got the second note right. Repeat this until you consistently play the notes correctly.

Once you're confident with two notes, increase the challenge to three notes, still starting with D and imagining the piano notes as you sing. Work on this until you can consistently play back what you've sung. When you can sing three notes accurately, this will form a short melodic idea!

When you're comfortable move on to four notes and see how far you can go.

Exercise Three – Sing and Play a Phrase

Now, try singing a simple musical Dorian phrase starting on the D note, that contains at least two notes and has some sort of rhythmic variation to make it more interesting. Sing while visualising playing it on the piano, then play it back to see how accurate you were. Begin with simple ideas and, as your confidence grows, extend the length of your phrases.

Once you're comfortable starting on D, try starting phrases on other notes within the Dorian mode. Repeat this later with Mixolydian and Lydian, but stay with Dorian for now.

Exercise Four – Sing a Solo

Away from the piano, sing a solo over the D Dorian mode backing track provided, while you visualise where the notes fall on the keyboard. This will help internalise your musical ideas. Whenever possible, record your sung solo with the backing track, then learn to play part or all of it on the piano.

You don't necessarily need a backing track for this exercise – you can sing in your head while imagining playing the notes while you're travelling, or even during a dull meeting!

Exercise Five – Write What's in Your Head

When you have completed the first four exercises with Dorian, Lydian, and Mixolydian, try this:

Imagine some simple licks in your head and, without touching the piano, write them on some blank music paper.

Write three licks for each mode, ensuring they are simple and melodic. Once you've written them, try playing them on the piano.

- Write three D Dorian licks over a Dm7 chord

- Write three G Mixolydian licks over a G7 chord

- Write three C Lydian licks over a Cmaj7 chord

Exercise Six: Solos With Backing Tracks

Play solos using the backing tracks provided for D Dorian, C Lydian, and G Mixolydian using only your right hand. Try to play what you hear in your head and sing along as you play. Many pianists, such as Keith Jarrett, sing while playing their solos. Doing this helps to create a strong connection between what you're thinking and what you're playing.

You might not be perfectly accurate all the time, but the more you practice, the better you'll become. Enjoy the process!

Chapter Ten: Left Hand Concepts in Modal Playing

The use of the left hand in modal jazz soloing has evolved in a distinctive way, and in this chapter we'll focus on what the left hand can play during extended one-chord vamps. In this chapter and Chapter Eleven, we'll be focusing our studies on the Dorian mode. We'll look specifically at the left hand techniques pioneered by McCoy Tyner, which have become synonymous with modal jazz piano.

To understand how McCoy Tyner developed his ideas, we first need to revisit Miles Davis' *Kind of Blue* album and the track *So What*. The way pianist Bill Evans arranged his chord voicings on this Dorian tune introduced the germ of an idea that later became the foundation for a whole new style of jazz piano chord voicings – so much so that they are now known as "So What" chords.

This way of arranging a chord is known as a *quartal voicing*. Take a look at how the Dm7 is played in the example below and use these voicings to play along to the original recording of *So What*. Can you see why they are called quartal voicings?

Example 10a

Quartal Chords

In traditional Western harmony we stack notes in 3rds to form chords, but So What chords are primarily constructed from stacks of 4ths, hence the term "quartal". If you look at the left-hand notes you'll see that there are three notes spaced a 4th apart.

Example 10b

The Character and Possibilities of Quartal Chords

Quartal chords are often less harmonically specific than traditional triads. For example, a triad-based Dm7 chord includes the root, 3rd, 5th and 7th and this combination of notes is quite specific to the Dm7 chord.

When we construct a quartal version of Dm7, however, we get the root (D), the 11th (G), and the 7th (C). This is a much less a specific chord and can be seen as a collection of notes that could create *many* different sounds depending on different factors, such as what bass note you play under them, or what scale you play above them.

To understand this sound and how it can be used, we'll take the three-note quartal voicing below and move it through the Dorian mode in scale steps. What do you think of this sound?

Example 10c

While it still sounds like a Dm7, quartal voicings have a much more open sound. The idea of moving a chord voicing through a scale, as we've just done, works in modal harmony because we're not thinking so much of the harmonic function of the chord (where the II chord leads nicely into the V chord etc), but are more concerned simply with the sound that is created and the mood it brings to the music. We're simply using the quartal voicing as a selection of intervals to enrich the tonality we're playing over.

As we discovered in the previous chapter, there are no wrong notes in the Dorian mode, allowing us to play collections of notes in any configuration and move them through the mode. The pianist McCoy Tyner embraced this concept of shifting quartal chords around and crafted it into a dynamic style of playing that has hugely influenced many jazz pianists who followed.

Rhythm

We can be creative not just with the notes, but with the rhythms we use to play these quartal voicings too. Play this example along with the backing track several times, then experiment by playing your own combinations of D Dorian quartal voicings with various rhythms.

Example 10d

Grounding The Rhythm and Harmony

When you start shifting chords and rhythms in this way, it is important to give clear rhythmic and harmonic reference points, not only to your audience, but your band members too.

McCoy Tyner would often ground the harmony and rhythm by playing a strong root and 5th, low on the keyboard, on the first beat of the bar. This regularity provided a solid base from which to launch more exploratory passages.

In the next example, you'll see how combining low 5ths with quartal chords can create a dynamic accompaniment for your right-hand soloing and is typical of what a jazz pianist might play in the left hand while soloing in this style.

Example 10e

Modal Left-Hand Exercises

The following exercise will help you develop this left-hand accompaniment technique.

Repeat this two-bar pattern until you're confident that you've mastered it, then play it along with the backing track. When you can play it fluently, try to play it with your eyes closed! The transition from the low 5th to the quartal chords and back will be challenging, but mastering this movement is essential in maintaining an uninterrupted flow in your right-hand soloing without interruption.

Example 10f

Now let's extend this exercise slightly.

Example 10g

Repeat the exercise keeping the low 5ths, but experiment by using different combinations of quartal chords on top. Repeat these combinations until you're fluent, then try doing everything with your eyes closed.

Finally, play along with the backing track while freely using various combinations of quartal chords and rhythms. Keep your improvisations anchored by adding low 5ths on the first beat of the bar whenever you feel the need to stabilise the flow.

Practise until this becomes second nature, as you will only be able to solo freely in your right hand when the rhythm part is solid. We'll be introducing some right-hand techniques in the next chapter, so ensure you are well-prepared!

Chapter Eleven: A Pentatonic Approach to Modes

In this chapter, we're going to explore an approach to modal soloing that uses pentatonic scales. Most jazz pianists are familiar with the idea of pentatonic soloing, and it's always useful to take something you already know and use it in a new context to create a sophisticated sound without too much effort.

Pentatonic scales make it easier to construct long sequences of notes that have a strong structure and melody, and add intensity and excitement to your solos.

Once again, McCoy Tyner was a pioneer in this area and we're going to explore some of his typical right-hand ideas. You'll learn a lot by immersing yourself in Tyner's soloing techniques and those of the musicians who were influenced by him, such as Chick Corea. An important feature of Tyner's pentatonic soloing was his use of melodic sequences and patterns and we will be exploring those ideas to create our extended lines.

Pentatonic Scales within Modes

Hiding within any mode, you will find three different pentatonic scales. If you examine the notes of the D Dorian mode, for instance, you'll discover D Minor, A Minor and E Minor Pentatonic scales all contained within.

Scale	1	3	4	5	7
Dm Pentatonic	D	F	G	A	C
Am Pentatonic	A	C	D	E	G
Em Pentatonic	E	G	A	B	D

In the next table, the notes of these scales are written below the notes of D Dorian, so you can see them in context. I've highlighted the root note of each pentatonic scale in bold.

Scale	Notes in D Dorian						
D Dorian	D	E	F	G	A	B	C
Interval	1	2	3	4	5	6	7
Dm Pentatonic	**D**		F	G	A		C
Am Pentatonic	D	E		G	**A**		C
Em Pentatonic	D	**E**		G	A	B	

Example 11a shows the D Minor Pentatonic scale embedded in the D Dorian mode.

Example 11a

D minor Pentatonic within the D Dorian mode (two octaves)

D   F   G   A   C   D   F   G   A   C   D

Here is a quick example of how the D Minor Pentatonic scale can be used over a D Dorian groove in a solo.

Example 11b

Next, here is the E Minor Pentatonic scale embedded in the D Dorian mode.

Example 11c

E minor Pentatonic within the D Dorian mode (two octaves)

E   G   A   B   D   E   G   A   B   D

Now, let's play an E Minor Pentatonic version of the lick in Example 11b over the D Dorian harmony. Play Example 11b and Example 11d side by side, to compare their sounds and get used to the character of different pentatonic scales.

Example 11d

Now, let's see the A Minor Pentatonic scale embedded within the D Dorian mode.

Example 11e

A minor Pentatonic within the D Dorian mode (two octaves)

Let's play the same lick again, but this time using A Minor Pentatonic over D Dorian.

Example 11f

You'll notice that each of these pentatonic scales brings its own unique character to the Dorian mode. When soloing for an extended period over one chord, alternating between different pentatonic options can maintain interest, as each scale offers a slightly different flavour.

Pentatonic Patterns

It's useful to develop a repertoire of small pentatonic "cells" (short musical phrases) that can combine to create extended musical lines.

One way to do this is to take a small motif and repeat it on ascending notes of the pentatonic scale. Here's an example ascending the D Minor Pentatonic scale.

Example 11g

Similarly, you can apply the same method descending.

Example 11h

Longer Exercises

The following ascending and descending patterns use all three of the minor pentatonic scales we've discussed and will help you become familiar with their shapes and the sounds they create over the D Dorian mode.

I've laid out the three pentatonic scales side by side within each exercise to help you get used to switching between them. However, to keep the examples manageable, I have separated the ascending and descending versions.

Example 11i

D Minor Pentatonic

A Minor Pentatonic

E Minor Pentatonic

Next, the descending versions.

Example 11j

D Minor Pentatonic

A Minor Pentatonic

E Minor Pentatonic

Let's repeat this process, this time with a four-note motif pattern. Here is the ascending version.

Example 11k

D Minor Pentatonic

A Minor Pentatonic

E Minor Pentatonic

And now the descending version.

Example 11l

Now let's play a descending three-note motif pattern that ascends.

Example 11m

5 A Minor Pentatonic

9 E Minor Pentatonic

And its converse: an ascending motif pattern that descends.

Example 11n

D Minor Pentatonic

5 A Minor Pentatonic

9 E Minor Pentatonic

We can extend this idea as before, using a four-note motif.

Example 11o

D Minor Pentatonic

A Minor Pentatonic

E Minor Pentatonic

Example 11p

D Minor Pentatonic

A Minor Pentatonic

E Minor Pentatonic

As you become more familiar with these pentatonic shapes and patterns, you'll begin to see the possibility of using more complex cells, which can be moved up/down the pentatonic scales. Try these examples, combined with the left-hand techniques we explored in the previous chapter.

Example 11q

Dm⁷ (D Dorian)

Example 11r

Example 11s

Example 11t

You will have noticed that the examples in this chapter are more like melodic patterns than traditional licks. These pentatonic patterns and others similar to them are like LEGO bricks and can be combined to create long, fluent, and dynamic modal lines.

As you become proficient, start to vary how you combine them in your playing. Mixing and matching them will make your lines sound fresh and interesting.

Learn a Solo

Listen to, study, and learn this solo to see how these pentatonic patterns can be effectively used. Notice especially how the lines transition between the three different minor pentatonic scales inside D Dorian, and notice how they are created by switching between various patterns.

The solo is played over the *So What* changes, so we modulate up to Eb Minor in the middle section before returning to D Minor. Don't be phased by this – it's everything you've learned already transposed up a half step.

Because the solo is played at a quicker tempo, feel free to work through it slowly to begin with in order to familiarise yourself with the phrasing. There's a lot to be gained from playing a left hand chord, then playing a right hand melody in free time, to really embed the sound of the scale in your ears. You can also, of course, isolate any phrase you particularly like and add that lick to your vocabulary of ideas, testing it out over other tunes you know.

Have fun working through it!

Example 11u

Now just enjoy jamming over the backing track in your audio download. Work on composing your own solos and see how creative you can be by combining the patterns you've learned in this chapter.

Also, spend time listening to McCoy Tyner and Chick Corea and try to identify some of the patterns they use in their soloing. Then see if you can bring some of their ideas into your own style. You don't have to copy their ideas perfectly, just try to grab a melodic shape and see what you can do with it.

Chapter Twelve: Bringing it All Together

The best way to understand and internalise any musical material is to hear it in action then apply it yourself, and this solo includes all the elements we've covered on our journey through this book.

Listen to this solo, learn it, and play it. Once you're done, complete the exercises at the end of the chapter to deepen your understanding of these concepts.

Example 12a

19 Fmaj7
D7
Gm7
C7
23 Fmaj7
Dm7
G7
27 Cmaj7
A7
Dm7
G7
31 Cmaj7
Em7(b5)
A7
Dm7
35

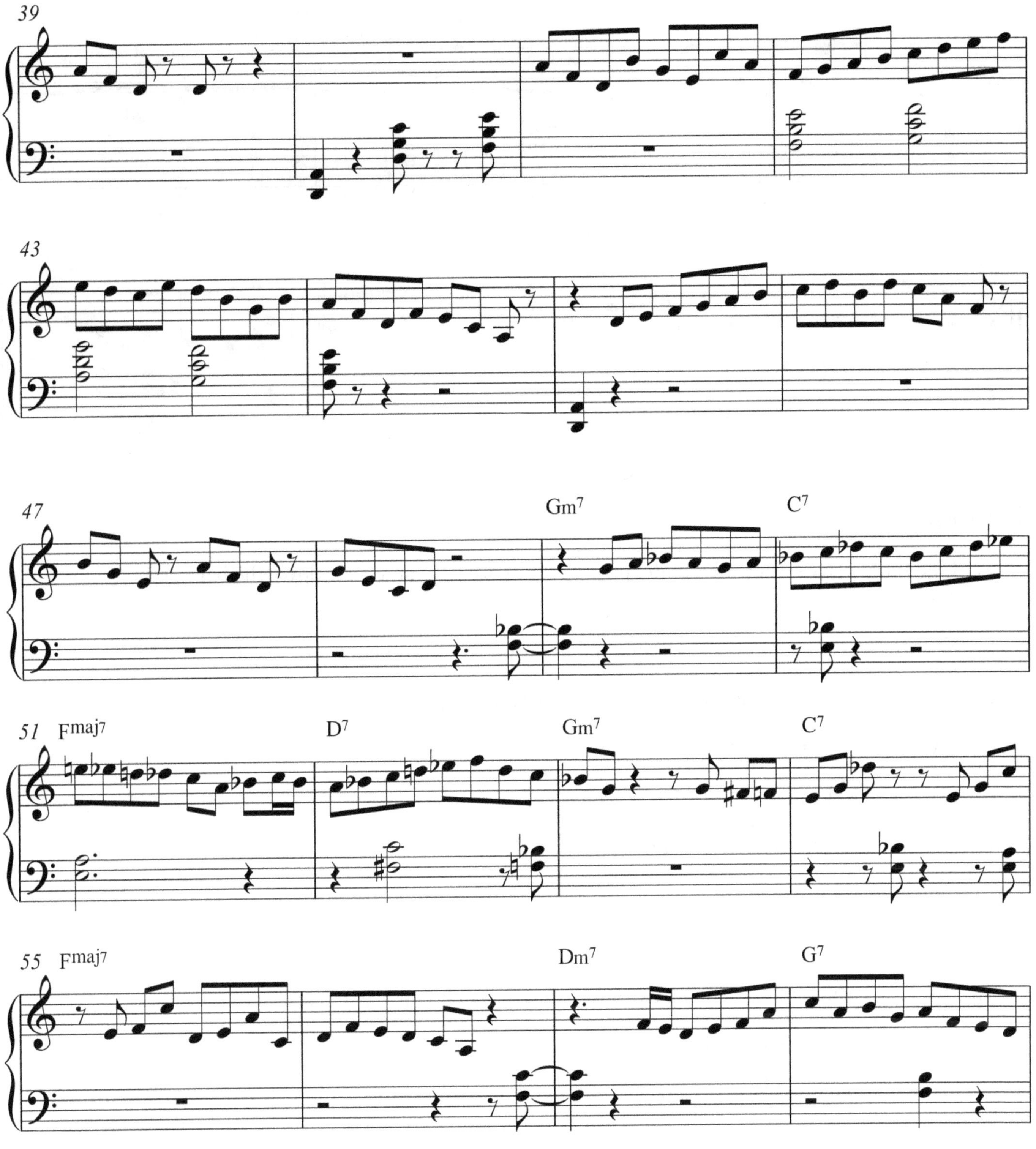
39
43
47
Gm7
C7
51
Fmaj7
D7
Gm7
C7
55
Fmaj7
Dm7
G7

Exercises:

1. Find three places where chromatic passing notes are used and write down the bar numbers: Bar_____, bar_____ and bar_____.

2. Write a lick using chromatic passing notes over a II – V – I chord progression.

3. Find and circle a 9th, an 11th, and a 13th over a Dm7 chord

4. Write a lick over Dm7 that includes a 9th, 11th and 13th.

5. Find and circle a b9, #11 and b13.

6. Write a lick using at least one altered extension.

7. Find a minor II – V – I.

8. Write a minor II – V – I lick.

9. Question: which mode is being used over the extended Dm7 sections?

10. Write a melodic sounding lick over Dm7.

11. Identify some pentatonic patterns being used in the long Dm7 sections.

12. Write a lick over Dm7 using one of the pentatonic patterns identified in the last question.

Conclusion

I want to encourage you to continue your learning journey with determination. Absorbing all the information in this book might take some time, but don't get discouraged. Keep revisiting your favourite licks, solos, and artists, and continue playing along to the backing tracks provided and jamming with anyone available.

Listen to the greats who speak this wonderful musical language and seize every opportunity to play with other jazz musicians. This will help you to become more fluent and increasingly able to express yourself to your satisfaction. Fluency and subtlety will develop gradually, allowing you to advance further.

Remember, learning licks and solos is a means to an end. The goal is to reach a point where all the licks, patterns, and stock phrases blend into each other, forming a vocabulary from which you can forge new and exciting ideas. It's at this stage that you start to feel you can truly express yourself through your soloing. You're beginning to get a good handle on the language.

Keep going and aim to progress further. In my next book, *Advanced Jazz Piano Soloing*, we'll explore more advanced harmonic concepts, chord voicings, solo jazz piano techniques, different keys, styles, and more.

Enjoy your playing!

Nathan